Quilting Design Treasury

by Anne Szalavary

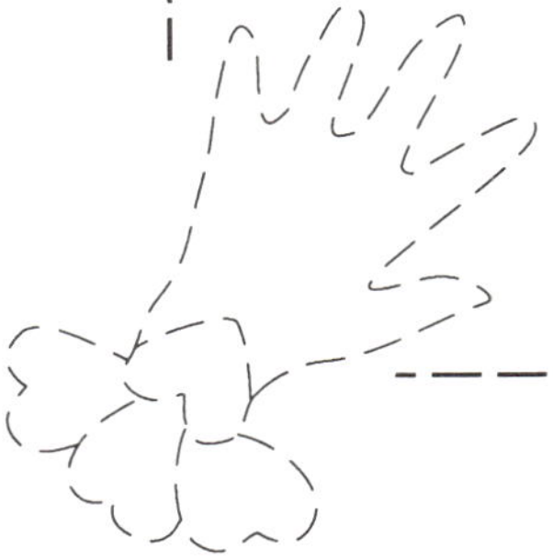

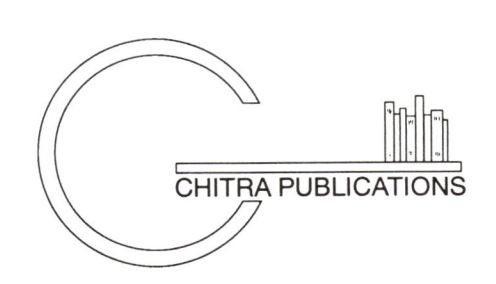

CHITRA PUBLICATIONS

Copyright ©1994 by Anne Szalavary

All Rights Reserved. Published in the United States of America.

Chitra Publications
2 Public Avenue
Montrose, Pennsylvania 18801

No part of this publication may be reproduced
or transmitted in any form or by any means, electronic
or mechanical, including photocopy, recording, or any information
storage and retrieval system now known or to be invented, without
permission in writing from the publisher, except by a reviewer who
wishes to quote brief passages in connection with a review written for
inclusion in a magazine, newspaper, or broadcast.

First printing: 1994

Library of Congress Cataloging-in-Publication Data
Szalavary, Anne.
    Quilting design treasury / by Anne Szalavary.
      p.   cm.
    ISBN 0-9622565-6-0 : $9.95
    1. Quilting--Patterns .   I. Title.
TT835 . S99 1994
746.46'041--dc20   94-11317
                                        CIP

Editorial Director: Patti Lilik Bachelder
Editor: Janice P. Johnson
Art Director: Diane M. Albeck

INTRODUCTION

uilting the backing, batting and quilt top together with pretty, decorative quilting designs is my favorite part of making a quilt. I love using my needle and thread to enhance a lovely patchwork or appliquéd design. As you work the designs, you will establish your own rythmn and pattern, and this is what makes your quilt a unique personal expression.

I still like to mark my quilt tops the old-fashioned way, transferring the design by the prick and pounce method which uses a needle inserted in a cork handle to pierce a design through paper, and powder to mark the design. Sometimes the best way is simply to set the pattern page beside the quilt and either draw the design by eye with washable marker or follow the design and quilt freehand. This will result in different interpretations of the patterns by each quilter as each one will express specific individual flourishes. Perhaps you'll want to add some extra lines to the design, or a touch of echo quilting by working around the entire outline a few times or many times to form concentric waves.

Whether you are a beginner or an advanced quilter, a veritable cornucopia of ideas and combinations awaits you. Colors and textures will come alive as you quilt the leaves, flowers, seashells, and butterflies. Quilting is the crowning touch to your work of art!

DEDICATION

For Joe, Jackie and Amanda Anne Marie, With Love.

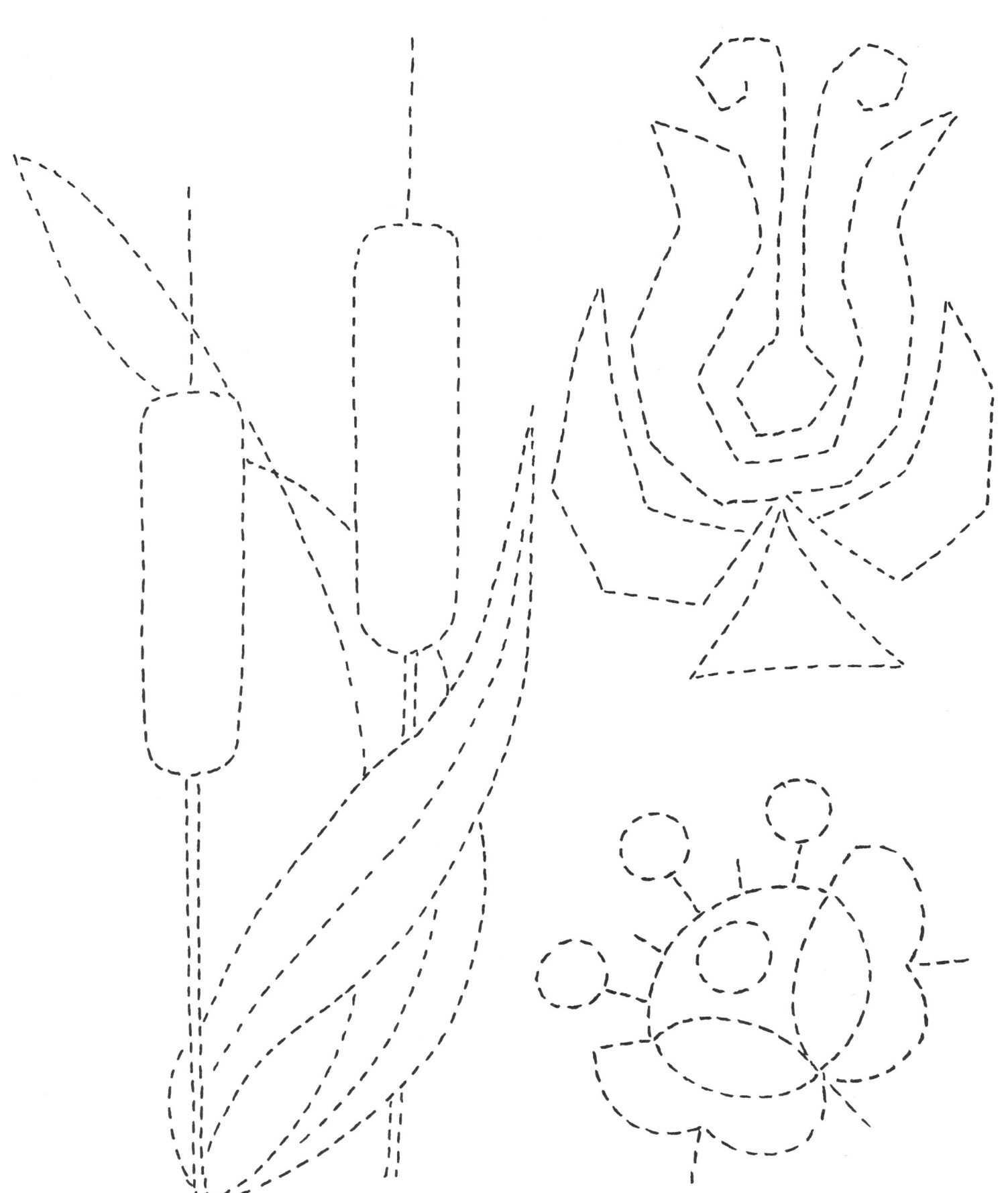

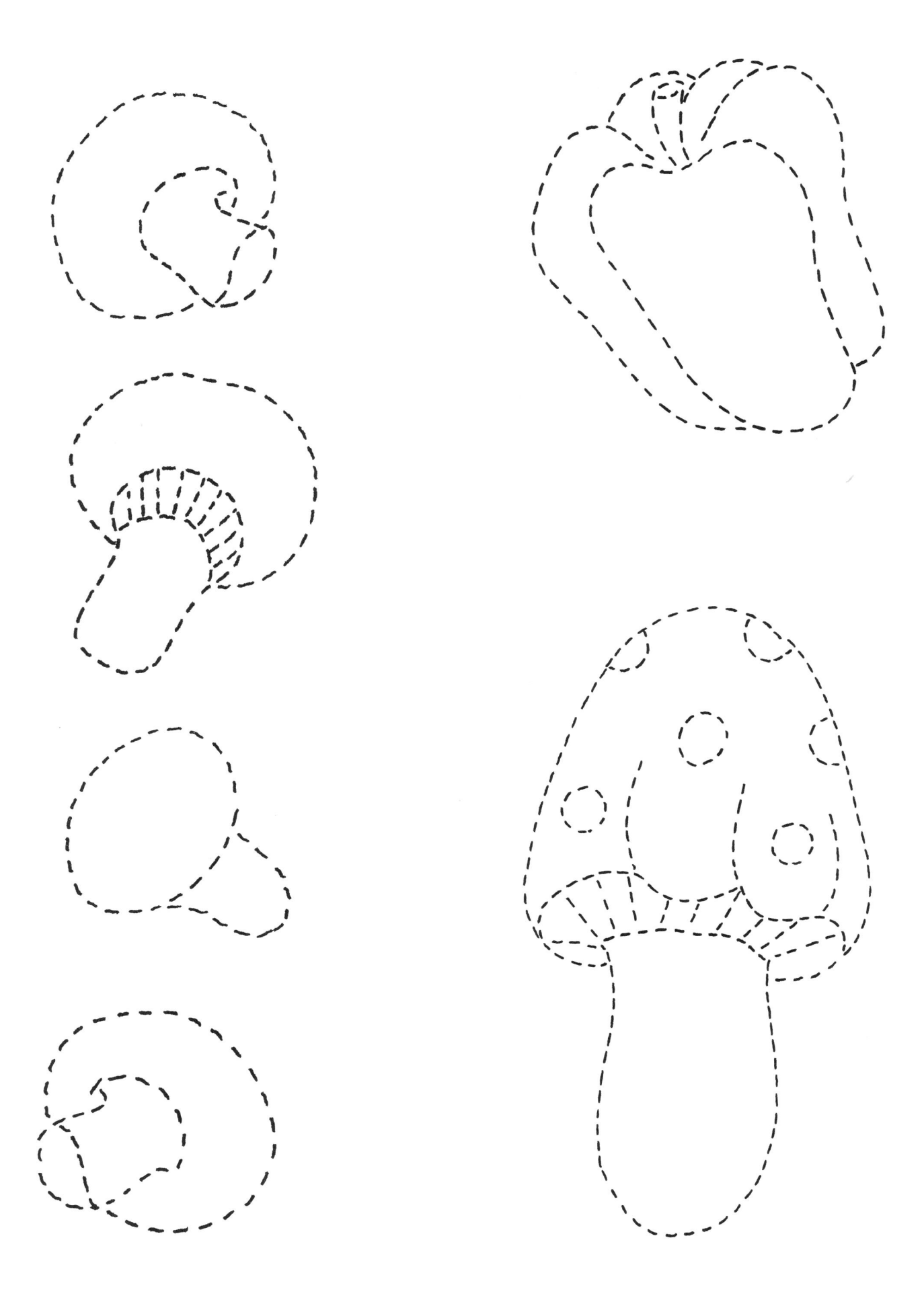

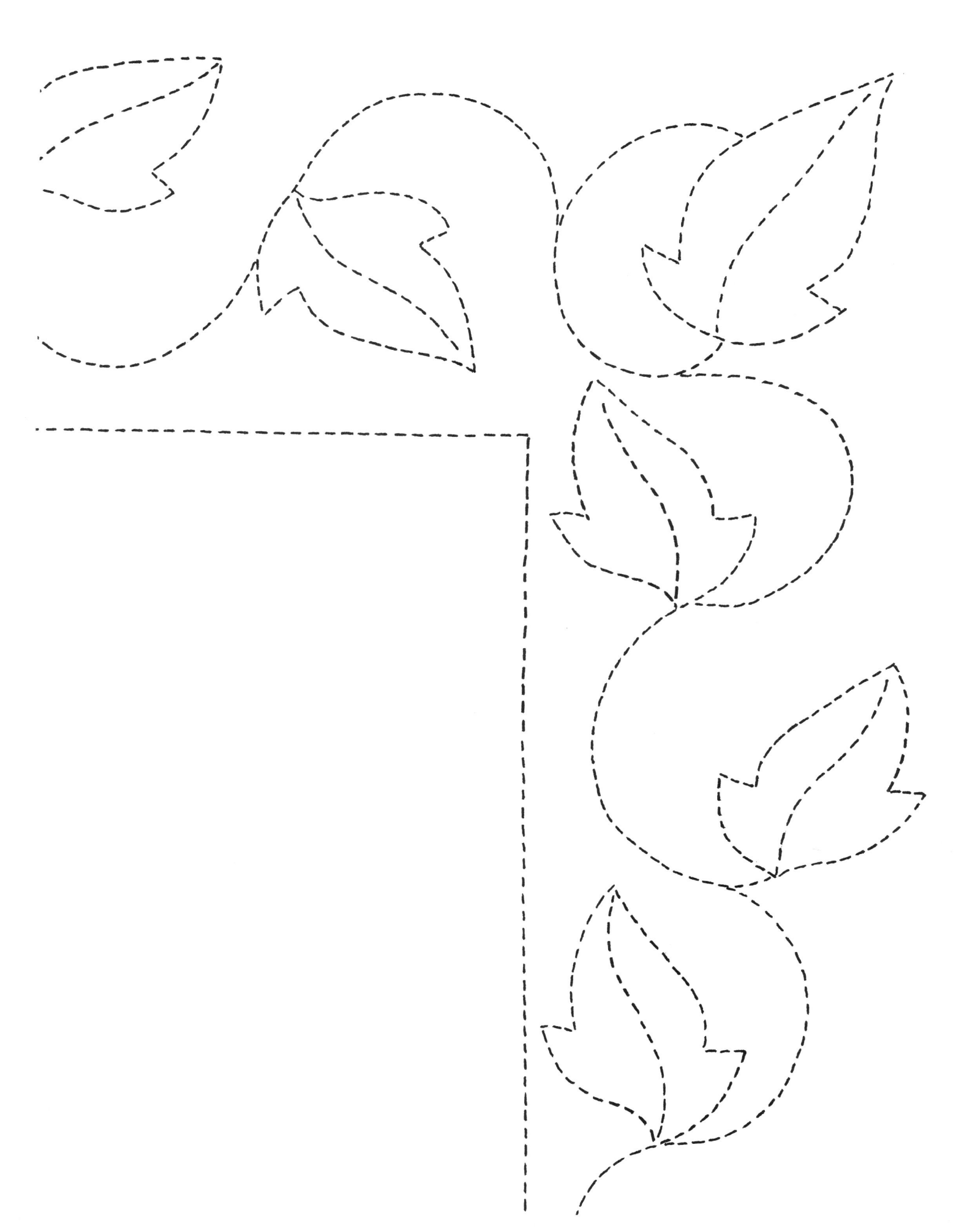

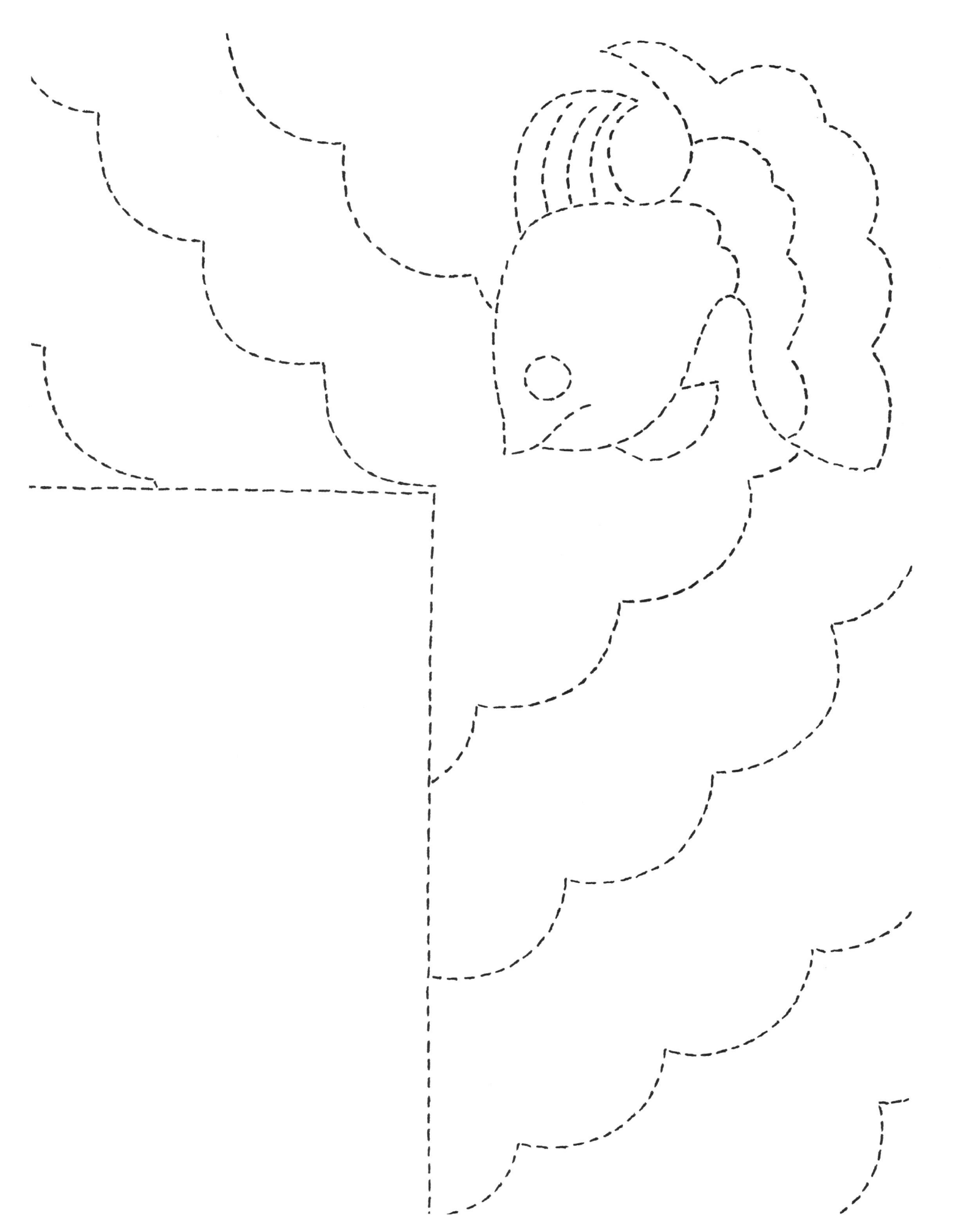

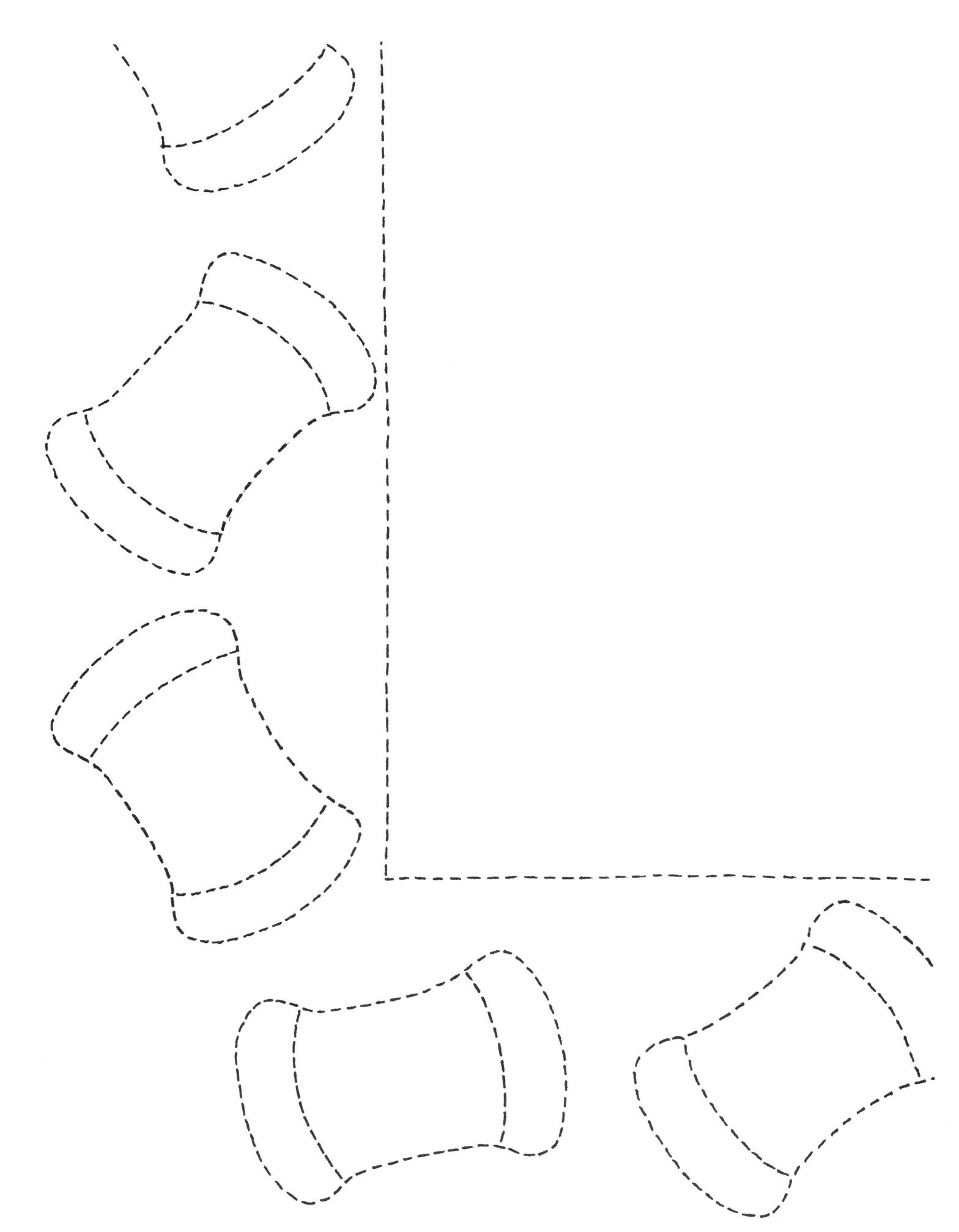

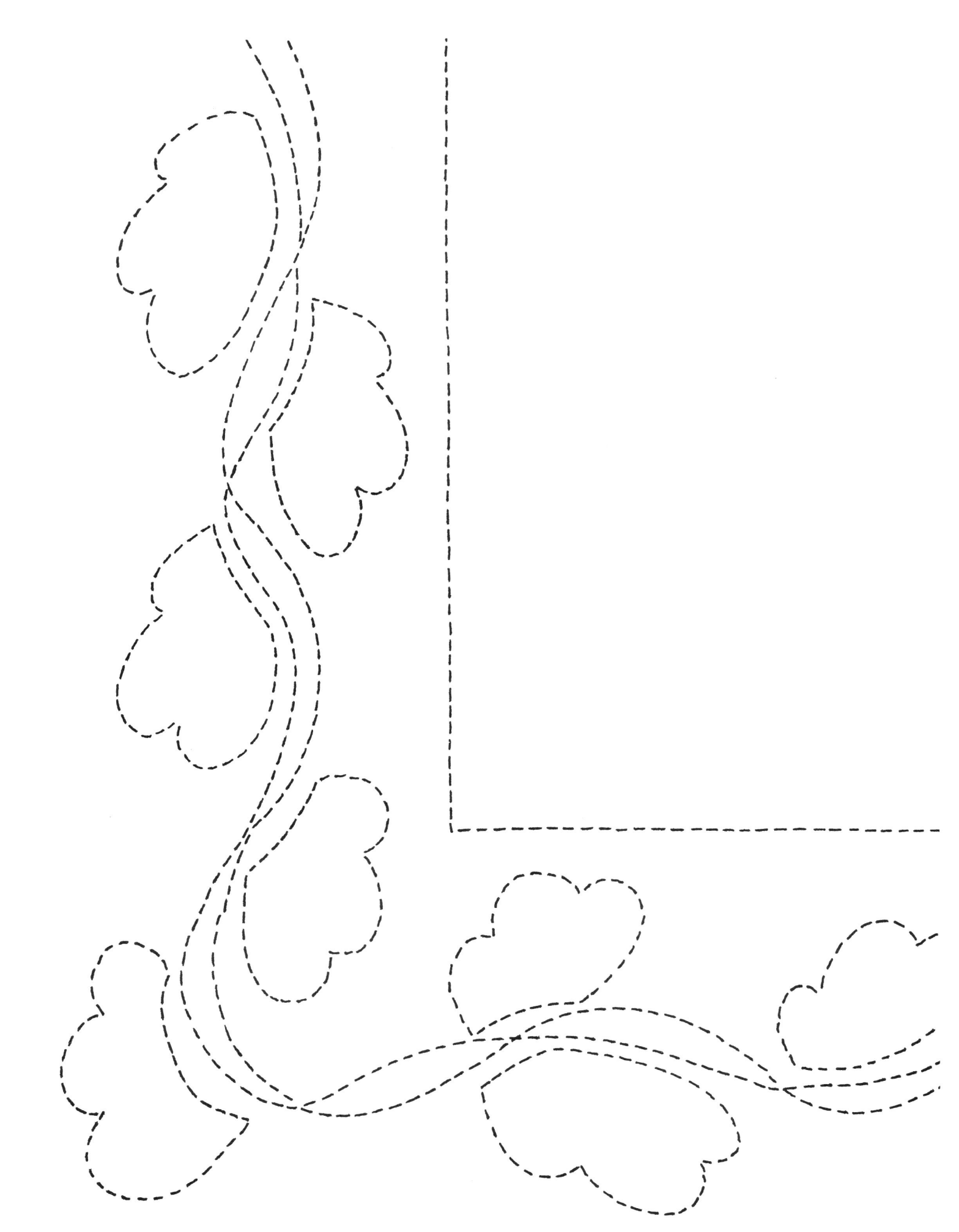

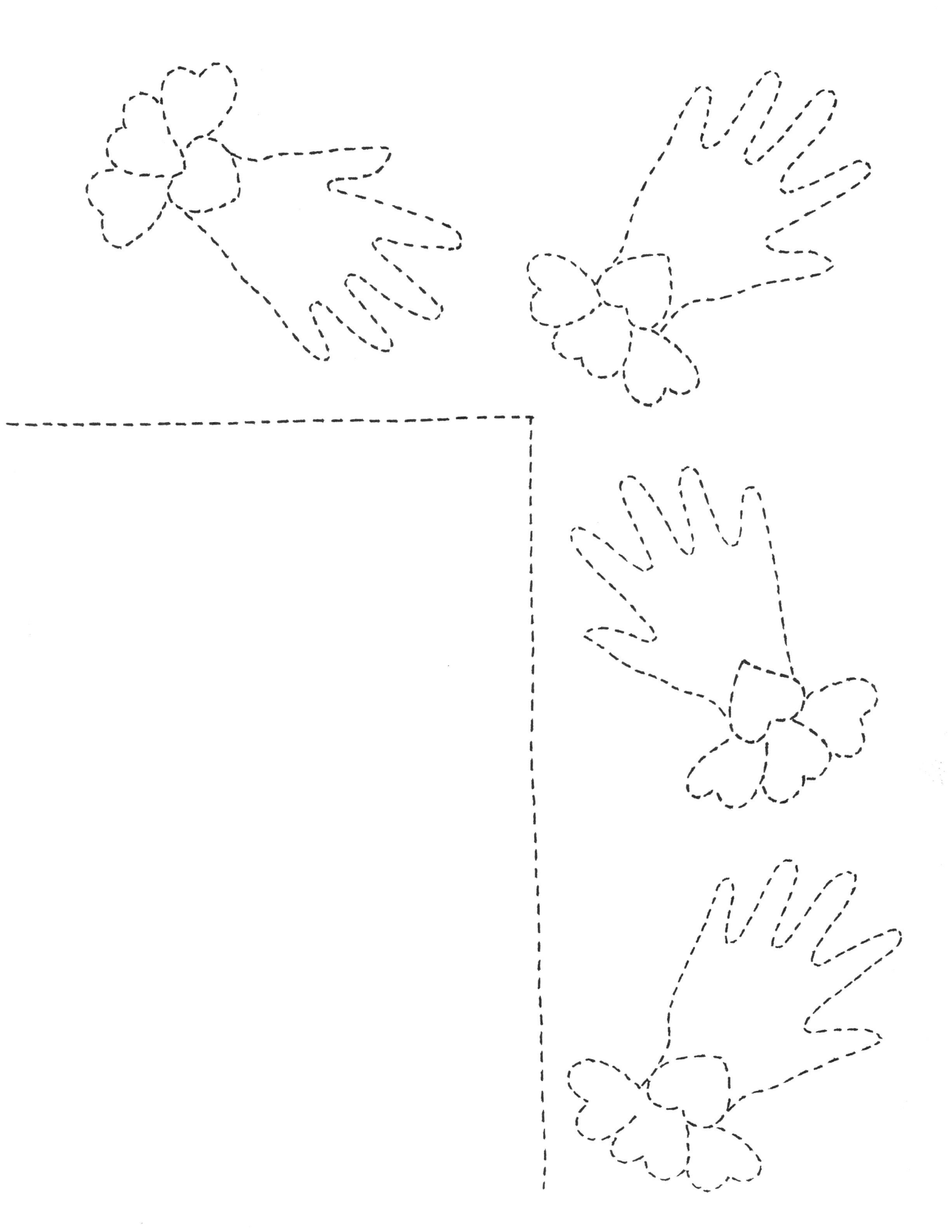

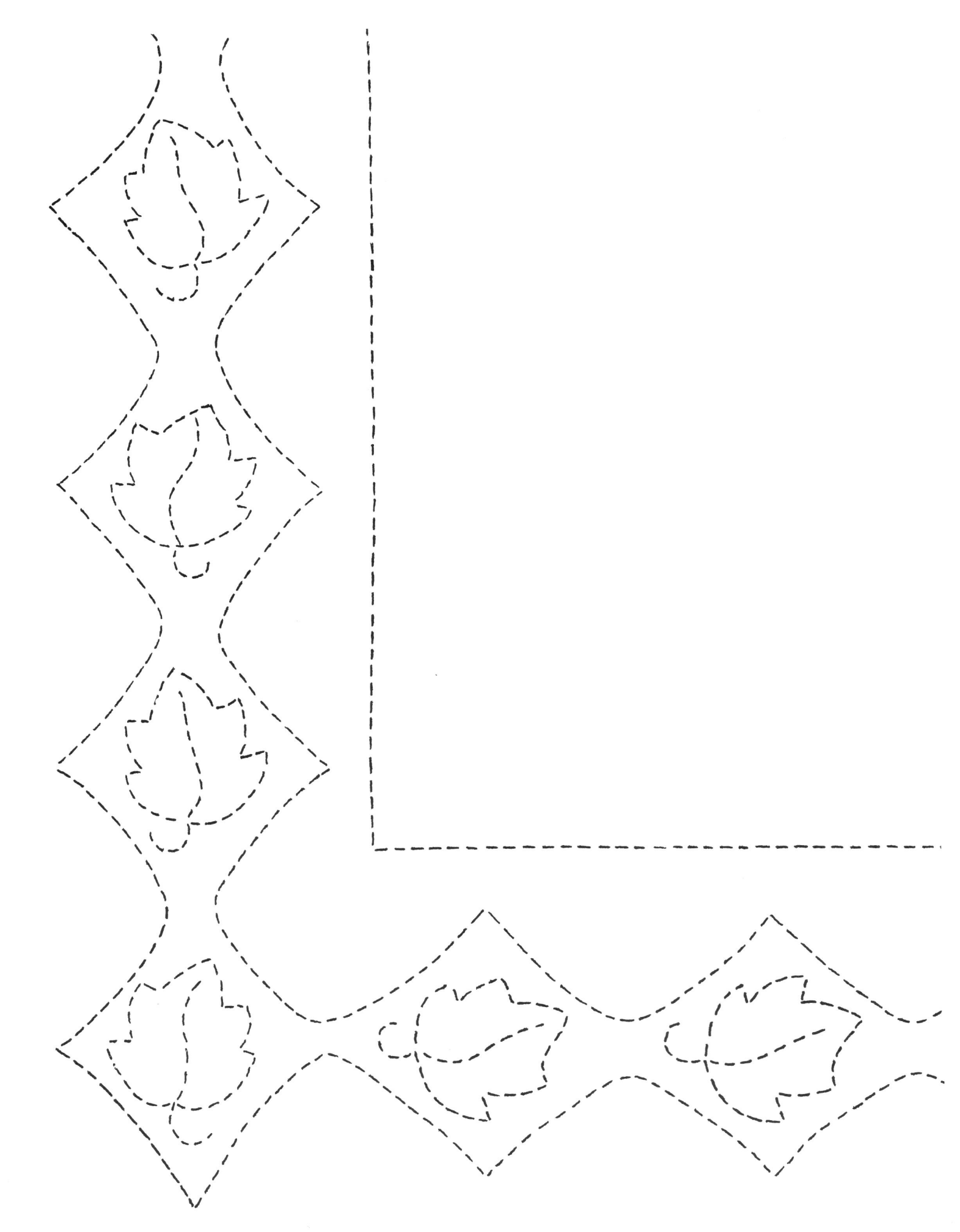

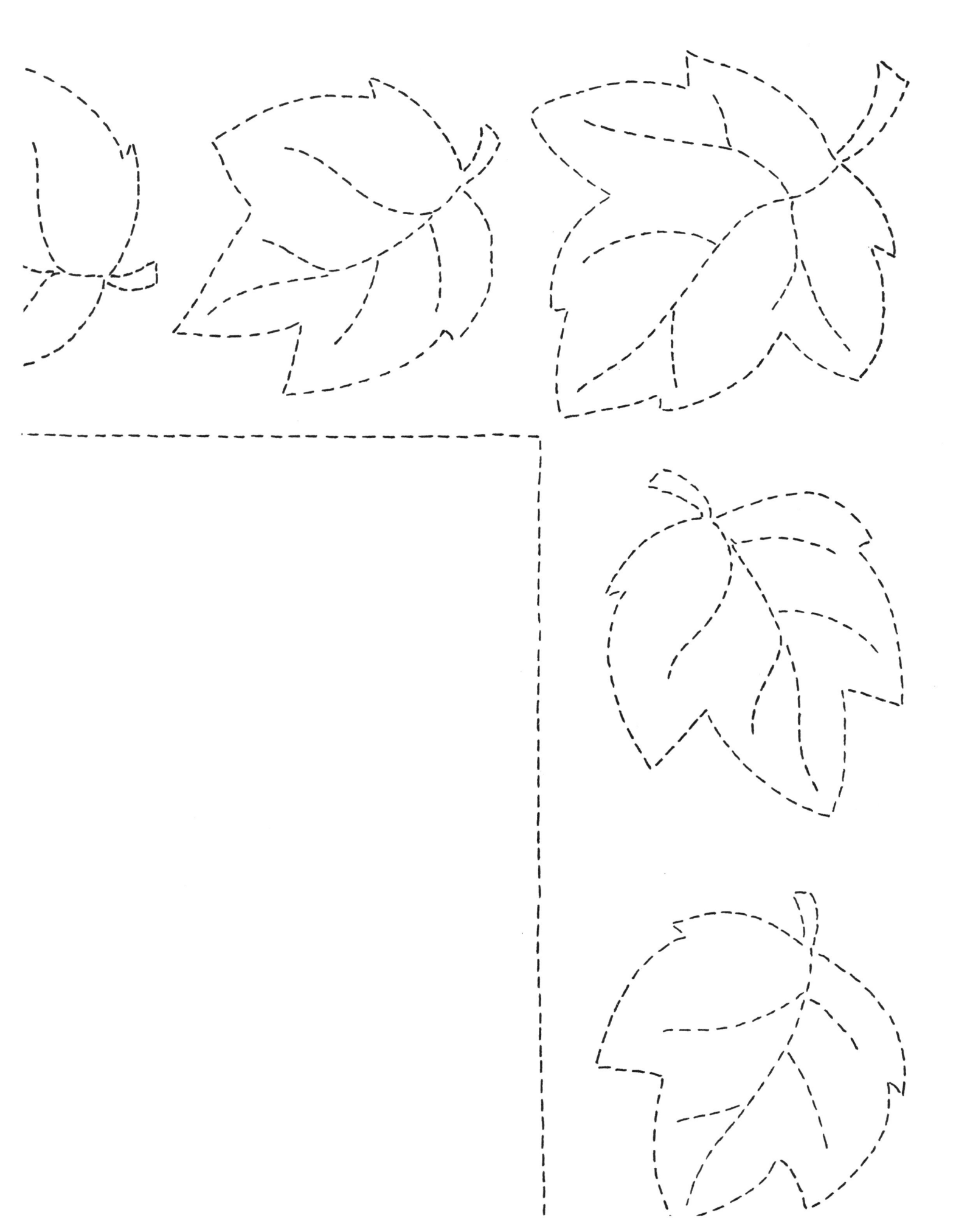

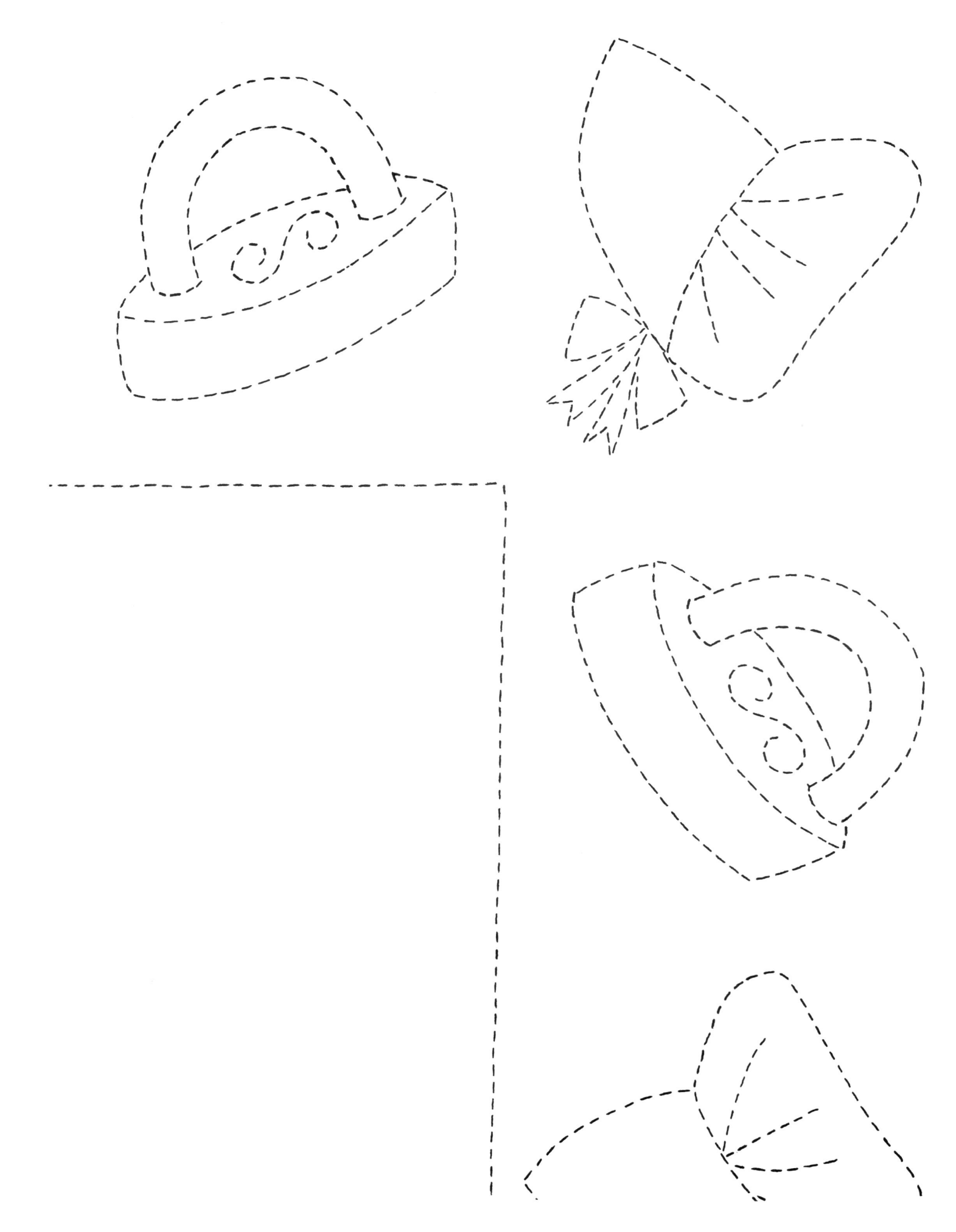

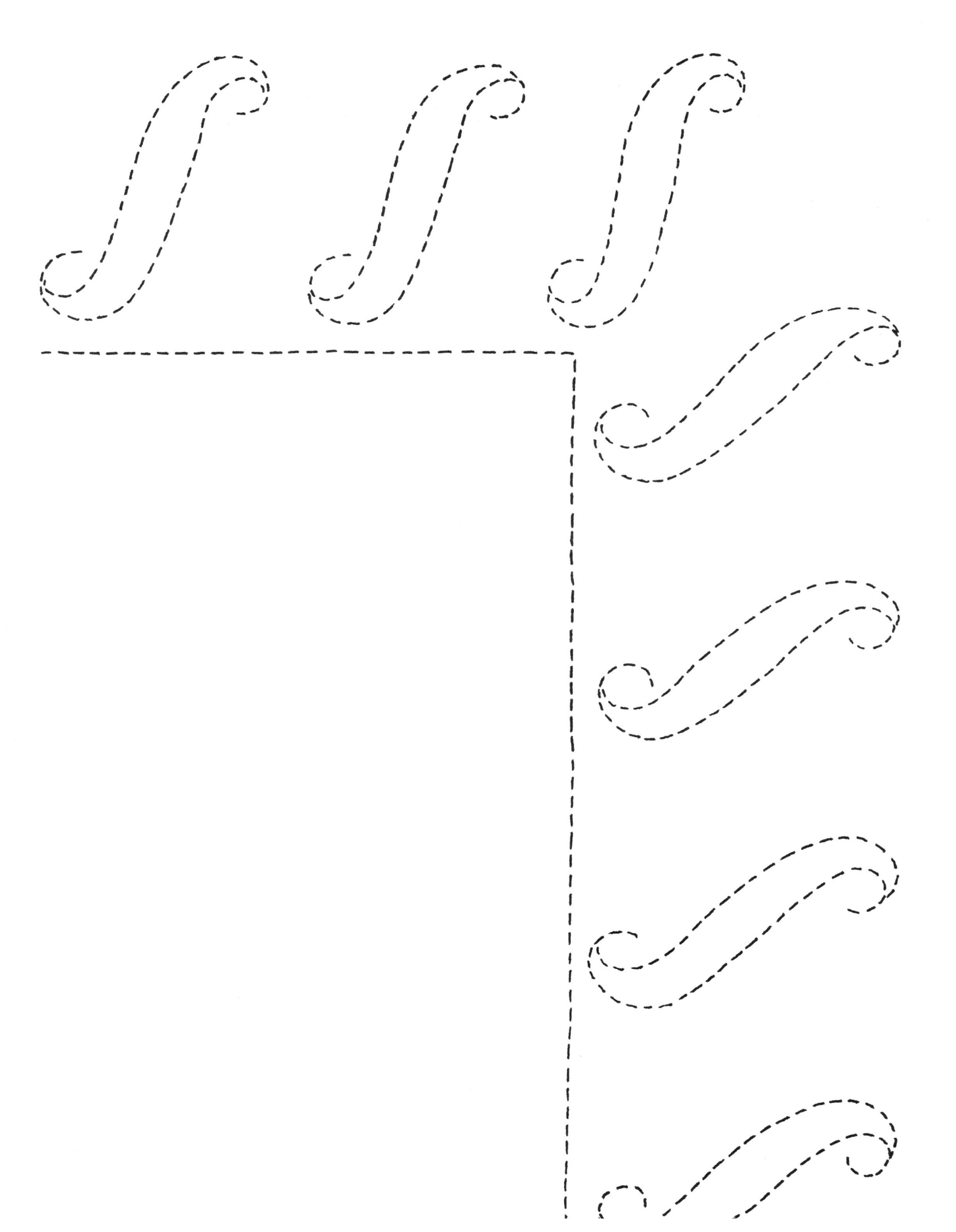

Also by Chitra Publications...

Magazines

Miniature Quilts • *Traditional Quiltworks*
Quilting Today • *Vegetarian Gourmet*

For subscription information, write to Chitra Publications, 2 Public Avenue, Montrose, PA 18801, or call 1-800-628-8244

Books

The Best of Miniature Quilts, Volume 1 compiled by Patti Lilik Bachelder
Designing New Traditions in Quilts by Sharyn Squier Craig
Drafting Plus: 5 Simple Steps to Pattern Drafting and More! by Sharyn Squier Craig
Small Folk Quilters by Ingrid Rogler
A Stitcher's Christmas Album by Patti Lilik Bachelder
Tiny Traditions by Sylvia Trygg Voudrie

Available in 1994:
Tiny Amish Traditions by Sylvia Trygg Voudrie
Theorem Appliqué: Abundant Harvest (Book I of IV) by Patricia B. Campbell and Mimi Ayers, Ph.D.
Luscious Low-Fat Desserts by Marie Oser

***Vegetarian Gourmet* Book Shoppe**

A convenient mail order resource for the best in vegetarian cookbooks. For a complete list, write to *Vegetarian Gourmet* Book Shoppe, 42 Church Street, Montrose, PA 18801. Or call toll-free 1-800-628-8244 (M-F, 8-4:30 EST).

The Quilter's Treasure Box

A convenient mail order resource for drafting supplies, quilting tools and notions, note cards, books and stencils. For a complete catalog, write to The Quilter's Treasure Box, 42 Church Street, Montrose, PA 18801. Or call toll-free 1-800-628-8244 (M-F, 8-4:30 EST).

CHITRA PUBLICATIONS